The Living River

The Living River

THE ROMANCE,

HISTORY AND BEAUTY

OF OUR NATION'S WATERWAYS

Edited by Peter Seymour

♛ Hallmark Crown Editions

ACKNOWLEDGMENTS: "Streams" by Clinton Scollard from *The Nature Lover's Knapsack* by Edwin Osgood Grover, Copyright © 1927 by Thomas Y. Crowell Company, Inc., with permission of the publisher. "Dragon Boat" and "Fulton's Folly" from *River Boats of America* by Frank Donovan, Copyright © 1966 by Thomas Y. Crowell Company, Inc., with permission of the publisher. "Carry On, Old Man River" by Louis Rosché from *Old Man River* by Robert A. Hereford. Copyright 1942. Reprinted by permission of the publishers, The Caxton Printers, Ltd. "A Torrent Terrible to Behold" by Captain Clark by permission of the publisher, The Arthur H. Clark Company, from *Sacajawea, Guide and Interpreter of the Lewis and Clark Expedition*, by Grace Raymond Hebard. Copyright 1932. "The Intimate Involvement" from *Rivers, Man and Myths* by Robert Brittain. Reprinted by permission of Curtis Brown, Ltd. Copyright © 1958 by Robert Brittain. "Mermaids" from *George Catlin and the Old Frontier* by Harold McCracken. Copyright © 1959 by Harold McCracken. Reprinted by permission of the publisher, The Dial Press. "Rivers Are Your Friends" from *Many Rivers* by Lewis R. Freeman. Copyright 1937. Reprinted by permission of the publishers, Dodd, Mead & Company. "Angler" from "Song of the Angler" by A.J. McClane in *Field & Stream* (October 1967). Reprinted by permission of *Field & Stream*. "River Dandies" from Chapter II of *Show Boat* by Edna Ferber. Copyright 1926 by Edna Ferber. Copyright renewed 1954 by Edna Ferber. All Rights Reserved. "What Has This Economy Wrought?" from pp. xiii-xiv of *Water Wasteland: Ralph Nader's Study Group Report on Water Pollution* by David Zwick and Marcy Benstock. Copyright © 1971 by The Center for Study of Responsive Law. Reprinted by permission of Grossman Publishers. "River Moons" from *Smoke and Steel* by Carl Sandburg, copyright, 1920, by Harcourt Brace Jovanovich, Inc.; renewed, 1948, by Carl Sandburg. Reprinted by permission of the publishers. "Ol' Man River" from *Show Boat* by Jerome Kern. Copyright 1928. With permission of the publisher T.B. Harms Company, New York, N.Y. "Forest Passage" from p. 138 "Along the channel... along the current" from *The Romance of the Rivers* by John T. Faris. Copyright 1927 by Harper & Row, Publishers, Inc., renewed 1955 by Bethann Faris Van Ness. Reprinted by permission of the publishers. "River's End" from *As the Sun Shines* by Henry Williamson. Copyright 1933 by Henry Williamson, renewed 1961 by Henry Williamson. Reprinted by permission of the author. "Mike Fink and Petticoat Peg" from *Mike Fink, King of the Mississippi Keelboatmen* by Walter Blair and Franklin J. Meine. Copyright 1933 by Holt, Rinehart and Winston, Inc. Copyright © 1961 by Walter Blair and Franklin J. Meine. Reprinted by permission of Holt, Rinehart and Winston, Inc. "The Once and Future Wilderness" from *The Colorado* by Frank Waters. Copyright 1946 by Frank Waters. Reprinted by permission of Holt, Rinehart and Winston, Inc. "American Primitive" from *The St. Lawrence* by Henry Beston. Copyright 1942 by Henry Beston. Copyright © 1970 by Elizabeth Coatsworth Beston. Reprinted by permission of Holt, Rinehart and Winston, Inc. "You Meet All Kinds on the River" from *The Monongahela* by Richard Bissell. Copyright 1952 by Richard Bissell. Reprinted by permission of Holt, Rinehart and Winston, Inc. "Kennebec: River Dying" from *Kennebec* by Robert P. Tristram Coffin. Copyright 1937 by Robert P. Tristram Coffin. Copyright © 1965 by Robert P.T. Coffin, Jr., Margaret Coffin Halvosa, Richard N. Coffin, Mary Alice Wescott. Reprinted by permission of Holt, Rinehart and Winston, Inc. "River Seasons" from *The French Broad* by Wilma Dykeman. Copyright 1955 by Wilma Dykeman. Reprinted by permission of Holt, Rinehart and Winston, Inc. "White Water" from pp. 78-81 of *Deliverance* by James Dickey. Copyright © 1970 by James Dickey. Reprinted by permission of the publishers, Houghton Mifflin Company. "Rogue River Folk" by Charles Hillinger from *Los Angeles Times* (June 25, 1972 issue). Copyright, 1972 by the Los Angeles Times. Reprinted by permission. "The River Everlasting" by Ward Dorrance. Copyright Charles Scribner's Sons 1939. Renewal copyright © 1967 Ward Dorrance. Reprinted from *Where the Rivers Meet* by Ward Dorrance by the permission of Charles Scribner's Sons. "Pirates, Indians and Alligators" from *The Western Journals of Washington Irving*, Edited and Annotated by John Francis McDermott. Copyright 1944 by the University of Oklahoma Press. Reprinted by permission. "Louis Armstrong on the *Dixie Belle*" from *Swing That Music* by Louis Armstrong. Copyright 1936 by Louis Armstrong, renewed 1964 by Louis Armstrong. Published by David McKay Co., Inc. Reprinted by arrangement with the publisher. "Tubin' on the Apple River" by Charles Kuralt from the CBS News "On the Road" Series. Reprinted by permission of CBS News.

PICTURE CREDITS - Bettmann Archive, pages 24, 26, 27, 29, 42, 43, 44, 48, 52; Dennis Brokaw (National Audubon Society), page 25; Ed Cooper, back dust jacket; Culver Pictures, pages 30, 45, 46-47, 50, 51, 54, 55; Dr. E.R. Degginger, page 71; Richard Fanolio, end papers, pages 4-5; Tony Florio (National Audubon Society), page 33; Dick Gunn, page 16; Grant Heilman, front dust jacket, title page (R), pages 18, 68, 69; Maxine Jacobs, pages 8-9, 72; Cooper Jenkins, title page (C); Robert Largent, page 49; Tom Myers, page 75; National Audubon Society, page 32; Larry Nicholson, pages 6-7, 10, 13, 62, 66, 67; Ed Simpson, title page (L); Charles Steinhacker, page 15 (L); Dan Sudia (National Audubon Society), page 15 (R); Arthur Tress, page 74; Larry West, page 14; Jack Zehrt, pages 11, 17, 20-21, 40-41, 56, 59, 60-61, 64, 65, 76.

Set in Bookman.
Printed on Hallmark Crown Royale Book paper.
Designed by William Hunt.

Introduction

This is a book of many voices, many views: a nature book, a history book, a nostalgic volume, an ecological edition. It contains the recollections, observations, and opinions of men and women who have lived over the last two centuries. Its theme is simply the river itself, and like a river it turns and twists, moves slowly and quietly or with speed and raucousness, is at times deep or shallow, has many tributaries, sings and growls, laughs and cries. In the end, I think, the book becomes much more than the sum of its parts. Which is what must be said of the river, too.

The river...it is water moving from source to outlet, moving always, never still; and so we have given rivers a human quality, and we have also made them symbolic of the course of human existence. But we cannot turn a river into a symbol and personify its motion, except poetically. For a river — its water, its channel, its movement from here to there — is essential to life, and without rivers there would be no life as we know it.

A river and the land around it comprise what is known as a watershed. This is a *natural community* — trees, plants, animals, insects. The river supports the life of the community. In the larger sense, the river supports the history of civilization. Henry Seidel Canby writes: "Rivers are dynamic, even the quietest. They make a road and a living place for men. They give them power to use, they create trade, they invite battles, they determine, in some degree, the quality of cultures. More than any other agency of nature, they make the earth usable by man."

It is impossible in this volume to praise individually all the rivers of the United States. If your own river is not mentioned, it is not because the river is unworthy. The book is just too brief.

While rivers are individuals, like people, they fall into certain basic personality profiles. And rivers behave differently, like people, at different times and in different places. One may be much like another most of the time. The similarities as well as the diversity of rivers throughout America have been covered here, and so what you see in general in your own river, you will find mirrored in this book. The little twists, bends, shallows, scenic points — the idiosyncracies of your river — they may be missing. But who, after all, knows them better than you?

Along with recollections, anecdotes, descriptions, historic incidents, poetry and song, I have included naturalist and conservationist viewpoints as well. The temptation to make it a solely "ecological" book was not overcome lightly. But such a narrow scope could not have done justice to the living river. For the research and reading that took place before I made a final selection of pieces aroused many feelings — a multitude of good feelings, of course, but also those of sorrow and anger. And finally a very strong sense of hope.

Sorrow because the river as a setting for romance and adventure has almost faded from the scene. Anger because man has selfishly, if at times ignorantly, violated and exploited the rivers and left them sick and dying. And hope because we seem at last to have realized the causes of the illness and are taking steps to cure and preserve the health of our inland waterways. I felt hope, too, because of the inherent and ultimate power in the vast sweep of nature. I believe with Ward Dorrance: "The rivers will remain....They will reflect our stars. They will mirror our bridges. They will be swift until the last ice."

Peter Seymour

The River Beautiful

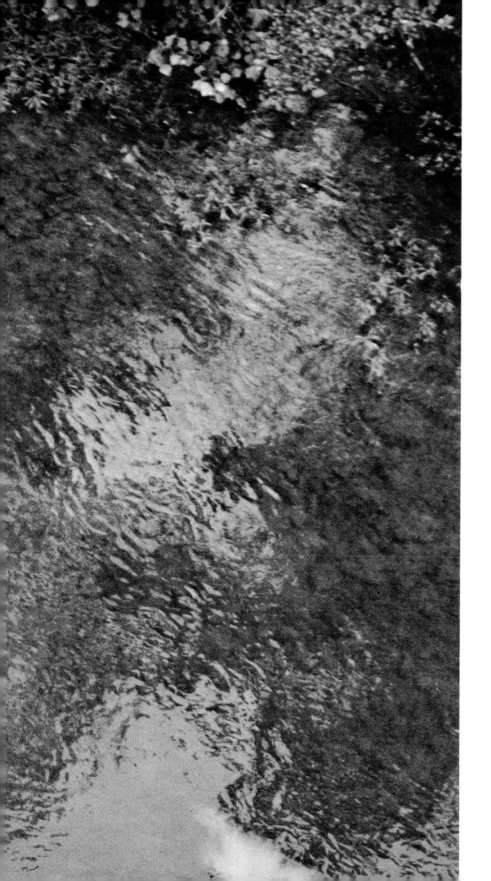

The Intimate Involvement

Man has furrowed and fenced the land, but to a large extent the great rivers remain untamed. Between man, the artisan, and the river, artless force of nature, there remains a spirit of accord aptly characterized by Robert Brittain as both wary and respectful.

Between men who change nature consciously and rivers whose work is witless, there is a deep affinity. It is a strange relationship, shifting and uncertain, established by men themselves in an infinite series of audacities and maintained at their own peril. They have never succeeded in taming the river as a dog is tamed, but neither have they ever been able to put it out of their minds. It has been teacher and slave, beast of burden, deified giver of life, demonic destroyer, scavenger — the relationship constantly changing as men themselves have changed. From the river men have drunk and lived, or they have drunk and died; from its sinuous body, ceaselessly moving yet remaining fixed, they have drawn their profoundest symbols of man's fate. Not yet fully used, never completely controlled, the river has been, of all natural forces, the one most intimately involved in human development at every stage.

River Seasons

Typical of many smaller rivers is the French Broad that runs across North Carolina and Tennessee. Wilma Dykeman shows us its yearly changes.

Which is the time to know the river? April along the French Broad is a swirl of sudden water beneath the bending buds of spicewood bushes, a burst of spring and a breath of sweetness between the snows of winter and the summer's sun. August is a film of dust on purple asters along the country roads of the lower river, and a green stillness of heavy shade splattered with sunlight beside the upper river. October is a flame, a Renaissance richness of red and amber, the ripeness of harvest in husk and bin. It is the golden span between the dry rattle of September's end and November's beginning.

Life's Stream

Henry David Thoreau in A Week on the Concord and Merrimack Rivers *observed not only the scenery but its significance as well.*

In the morning the river and adjacent country were covered with a dense fog, through which the smoke of our fire curled up like a still subtiler mist; but before we had rowed many rods, the sun arose and the fog rapidly dispersed, leaving a slight stream only to curl along the surface of the water.

We rowed for some hours between glistening banks trickling with water. Sometimes this purer and cooler water, bursting out from under a pine or a rock, was collected into a basin close to the edge of and level with the river. So near along life's stream are the fountains of innocence and youth making fertile its sandy margin; and the voyageur will do well to replenish his vessels often at these uncontaminated sources. As the evaporations of the river feed these unsuspected springs which filter through its banks, so, perchance our aspirations fall back again in springs on the margin of life's stream to refresh and purify it.

Streams

I so love water-laughter,
  Its bubbling flecks and gleams,
I pray in the hereafter
  There somewhere may be streams.

I'd have for my companion
  In some celestial nook,
Beneath a spreading banyan,
  The music of a brook.

Its measures would entice me,
  Uncumbered by the clay,
Its melody suffice me
  Till drooped the heavenly day.

Then its all-liquid laughter
  Would murmur through my dreams;
I pray in the hereafter
  There somewhere may be streams.

Clinton Scollard

12

Forest Passage

*Writing in 1785, John Filson evokes the serenity of the river and the
life it shares with the creatures of the forest.*

Along the channel of "the beautiful river" [the Ohio], severing the
dark forests on either side, like the zig-zag lightning's path through
the black clouds, they floated on the gentle current. The huge old
sycamores and cottonwoods that had beautified the wild banks for
untold years stood at the water's edge and leaned over the stream
and beheld their wide-spreading arms and giant forms mirrored in
the crystal waters. Everything along the shore indicated the unin-
terrupted abode of the wild animals of the forest, except here and
there, upon some rich bottom raised above the vernal floods, peeped
from the rank foliage solitary mounds that had been reared so long
ago by human beings that their builders had passed away without a
tradition, a history, or a name. The haughty buffalo, and the timid
deer, disdaining the smaller streams that paid tribute to the Ohio,
came to the margin of the main river to slake their thirst, and there
was nothing in all the vast solitude to remind me of civilized life except the rude vessel that floated along the current.

River Moons

The double moon, one on the high backdrop of the west,
   one on the curve of the river face,
The sky moon of fire and the river moon of water, I am
   taking them home in a basket, hung on an elbow, such
   a teeny weeny elbow, in my head.
I saw them last night, a cradle moon, two horns of a moon,
   such an early hopeful moon, such a child's moon for all
   young hearts to make a picture of.
The river—I remember this like a picture—the river
   was the upper twist of a written question mark.
I know now it takes many many years to write a river,
   a twist of water asking a question.
And white stars moved when the moon moved, and one red star
   kept burning, and the Big Dipper was almost overhead.

Carl Sandburg

The St. Lawrence emerges from Lake Ontario and flows northeasterly, forming part of the border between New York State and Canada, and empties at last in a vast opening into the sea. It is a proud river. Here Henry Beston tells its story.

A bold turn of a gravel promontory, and one escapes out of the caldron into a broading reach of calmer water. Widening, widening to a lake, the river achieves an afternoon peace, and there comes slowly into view a landscape so much part of the old beauty of the past, a landscape so poignantly and profoundly American, that time seems to have stood still awhile above the river.

Across the placidity of milk, this quiet of a steel engraving, the level shores seem farther away than they really are, and beyond their dreamlike fields and distant, unsubstantial woods blue mountains rise like painted shapes of the older line and mood. Even the few islands in sight are the islands one sees in the older American prints, each one trailing off downstream with a submerged spur from whose tall grasses the red-winged blackbirds rise. All sign and show of industrial perversion has melted from sight. It is the America of Audubon, the country of the *Last of the Mohicans.*

16

The Once and Future Wilderness

In his book The Colorado, *Frank Waters captures the everlasting mystical dimensions of a river that will likely never be "civilized."*

The Colorado is an outlaw. It belongs only to the ancient, eternal earth. As no other, it is savage and unpredictable of mood, peculiarly American in character. It has for its background the haunting sweep of illimitable horizons, the immensities of unbroken wilderness. From perpetually snow-capped peaks to stifling deserts below sea level, it cuts the deepest and truest cross section through the continent....

Its landscapes are never anywhere urban or commercial, not even pastoral. They are purely mystical in tone. There are the windswept rocky wastes high above timberline, the sunless gloom of deep gorges. When the river does rise to the surface again it is upon the face of an earth whose expressions are never twice the same....

Those who love it best are those who fear it most. For like all things touched with the sublime it carries a lurking horror, and its mysteries wear the mask of the commonplace. To allude to it as something more than a river would sound like a literary affectation only to the literary. The illiterate might well comprehend most fully all that it expresses. As from a Navajo sand painting or ceremonial blanket he would read the river's cryptic meaning in the earth it threads.

The dreamlike vacuousness, wild beauty and barbaric boldness of design form but the pattern of the warp which underlies the subtle, inimical resistance of the woof. Old, ancient America! With its own great spirit of place; with the shadows of aboriginal ghosts still gliding across it; and with its own demons not yet appeased — the haunting promise of the far-off, its tormenting unrest.

It is still a wilderness. To understand it you must think in new dimensions. You must feel in terms of depth as well as space, of eternity and not of time.

Consecration

More poetry than prose, here is one man's heartfelt tribute to the beautiful rivers.

It is by a river that I would choose to make love, and to revive old friendships, and to play with the children, and to confess my faults, and to escape from vain, selfish desires, and to cleanse my mind from all the false and foolish things that mar the joy and peace of living.

Henry van Dyke

River's End

Few of us have looked upon the river at its journey's end, seen here through the eyes of Henry Williamson.

The stream wound its way through the wasteland, coming at last to a gorge through the sandhills where the marram grasses and brambles made against the sky a fringe, quivering and seeming to dissolve in the heated air. The sea from an everlasting murmur became a refreshing roar, for the waves were coming quickly up the sands. Now the stream was preparing for its end, spreading wide and hurrying with multitudinous small leaps and cries over the stones of its delta. Here was its last bridge, of sea-eaten brown iron piles, supporting a footway of single planks. Every high tide altered the miniature estuary, which some days was narrow and at other times wide and noisy with its thousand stones washed and shifted anew, and the sand-cliffs of its banks collapsing noisily. Here a scour or sandbank arose, only to be cut away the next minute amidst a swirl that lifted the baby flatfish and showed their pallid undersides. Wider trickled the water, and more shallow. Now one might cross wearing shoes which would not be wetted above the welt. Gulls stood below on the wet sands; but now where was the water? Its brawling over, the summer stream was gone under the sand, to its immortality in the immense sea.

The Coming of Man to the River

CHARLES RUSSELL: *On the Flathead,* Thomas Gilcrease Institute, Tulsa, Oklahoma

Of the Great River Called Mississippi

Imagine yourself a stranger in a strange land making your way down forbidden waterways. Imagine then how bizarre our native spoonbill and 200-pound channel catfish must have seemed to explorer Jacques Marquette as he writes of this historic river.

Here we are, then, on this so renowned River, all of whose peculiar features I have endeavored to note carefully. The Mississippi River takes its rise in various lakes in the country of the Northern nations. It is narrow at the place where Miskous empties; its Current, which flows southward, is slow and gentle. To the right is a large Chain of very high Mountains, and to the left are beautiful lands; in various Places, the stream is Divided by Islands. On sounding, we found ten brasses of Water. Its Width is very unequal; sometimes it is three-quarters of a league, and sometimes it narrows to three arpents. We gently followed its Course, which runs toward the south and south-east, as far as the 42nd degree of Latitude. Here we plainly saw that its aspect was completely changed. There are hardly any woods or mountains; The Islands are more beautiful, and are Covered with finer trees. We saw only deer and cattle, bustards, and Swans without wings, because they drop Their plumage in This country. From time to time, we came upon monstrous fish, one of which struck our Canoe with such violence that I Thought that it was a great tree, about to break the Canoe to pieces. On another occasion, we saw on The water a monster with the head of a tiger, a sharp nose Like That of a wildcat, with whiskers and straight, Erect ears; The head was gray and The Neck quite black; but We saw no more creatures of this sort: When we cast our nets into the water we caught Sturgeon, and a very extraordinary Kind of fish. It resembles the trout, with This difference, that its mouth is larger. Near its nose — which is smaller, as are also the eyes — is a large Bone shaped Like a woman's busk, three fingers wide and a Cubit Long, at the end of which is a disk as Wide As one's hand. This frequently causes it to fall backward when it leaps out of the water.

A Torrent Terrible to Behold

A flash flood makes the river a brutal and sudden killer. Such a flood nearly claimed the life of Sacajawea, the guide of the Lewis and Clark expedition, her husband and infant son. Captain Clark narrates their brush with death.

I determined myself to proceed on to the falls and take the river; according we all set out. I took my servant and one man, Charbono our interpreter, and his squaw [Sacajawea] accompanied. Soon after I arrived at the falls, I perceived a cloud which appeared black and threatened immediate rain. I looked out for a shelter, but could see no place without being in great danger of being blown into the river if the wind should prove as turbulent as it is at some times. About one fourth of a mile above the falls I observed a deep ravine in which was shelving rocks under which we took shelter near the river and placed our guns, the compass, etc., etc. under a shelving rock on the upper side of the creek, in a place which was very secure from rain. The first shower was moderate, accompanied with a violent wind, the effects of which we did not feel. Soon after a torrent of rain and hail fell more violent than ever I saw before; the rain fell like one volley of water falling from the heavens and gave us time only to get out of the way of a torrent of water which was pouring down the hill into the river with immense force, tearing everything before it; taking with it large rocks and mud. I took my gun and shot pouch in my left hand, and with the right scrambled up the hill pushing the interpreter's wife [Sacajawea] (who had the child in her arms) before me, the interpreter himself making attempts to pull up his wife by the hand, much scared and nearly without motion. We at length reached the top of the hill safe, where I found my servant in search of us, greatly agitated for our welfare. Before I got out of the bottom of the ravine, which was a flat dry rock when I entered it, the water was up to my waist and wet my watch. I scarcely got out before it raised ten feet deep with a torrent which was terrible to behold and by the time I reached the top of the hill, at least fifteen feet of water. I directed the party to return to the camp at the run as fast as possible to get to our lode, where clothes could be got to cover the child, whose clothes were all lost, and the woman, who was but just recovering from a severe indisposition, and was wet and cold. I was fearful of a relapse. I caused her, as also the others of the party, to take a little spirits, which my servant had in a canteen...I lost at the river in the torrent the large compass, an elegant fusee, tomahawk, umbrella, shot pouch and horn with powder and ball, moccasins, and the woman lost her child's bier and clothes, bedding, etc.

The Horse-Yacht

River travel has known all shapes and forms, from the dugout canoe and ten-foot skiff to the ferry flats and Kentucky broadhorns — massive, thick-planked houseboats blundering through the river like derelict waterbugs. Yet, what Henry van Dyke calls a "horse-yacht" was surely the strangest and grandest craft of all.

Have you ever seen a horse-yacht? Sometimes it is called a scow; but that sounds common. Sometimes it is called a house-boat; but that is too English.

The foundation of the horse-yacht — if a thing that floats may be called fundamental — is a flat-bottomed boat, some fifty feet long and ten feet wide, with a draft of about eight inches. The deck is open for fifteen feet aft of the place where the bowsprit ought to be; behind that it is completely covered by a house, cabin, cottage, or whatever you choose to call it, with straight sides and a peaked roof....

The motive power of the yacht stood patiently upon the shore.... Three more pessimistic-looking horses I never saw. They were harnessed abreast, and fastened by a prodigious tow-rope to a short post in the middle of the forward deck. Their driver...sat upon the middle horse, and some wild instinct of colour had made him tie a big red handkerchief around his shoulders, so that the eye of the beholder took delight in him....

As soon as one learns to regard the horse-yacht as a sort of moving house, it appears admirable. There is no dust or smoke, no rumble of wheels, or shriek of whistles. You are gliding along steadily through an ever-green world; skirting the silent hills, passing from one side of the river to the other when the horses have to swim the current to find a good foothold on the bank. You are on the water, but not at its mercy, for your craft is not disturbed by the heaving of rude waves, and the serene inhabitants do not say, "I am sick." You may sleep, or read, or write in your cabin, or sit upon the floating piazza in an armchair and smoke the pipe of peace, while the cool breeze blows in your face and the musical waves go singing down to the sea.

CARL BODMER: *Tower Rock,* Thomas Gilcrease Institute, Tulsa, Oklahoma

Mike Fink and Petticoat Peg

Mike Fink, the fightingest, drinkingest, rowdiest man on five rivers, roved up and down the Sangamon, Ohio, Mississippi, Missouri, and Yellowstone rivers and their tributaries. Called the King of the Keelboatmen, Mike's prowess became legendary. And, as revealed in this account by his biographer, Walter Blair, Mike had a way with the ladies.

One night in November, 1820, Mike's keelboat joined a number of keels which had tied up just below the broad mouth of the Muskingum River. After making all fast, Mike, just under the bank, scraped together a heap of the dry brown beach leaves which the winds of autumn were fluttering to the ground. Curious boatmen gathered around.

"Building a house, Mike?"

"Out of chawing tobaccy?"

"Goin' to feed your keelboat?"

Mike made no reply; he continued his work until he had heaped the leaves head high. Then he separated the leaves, making them into an oval. Thoughtfully, he spread his body in the hollow in the center, as if he were interested in finding out whether or not the leaves made a comfortable bed. Rising, he climbed aboard the boat, found his rifle, ostentatiously primed it, and then sternly shouted, "Peg!"

Dressed in homespun, a fine red kerchief about her brown neck, her feet bare, a red-cheeked girl, who may or may not have been Mike's wife, emerged from the dusk of the cargo box. She followed the scowling boatman, after a curt demand, to the structure of leaves, anxiously trying to study his face.

"Damn you, get in there and lay down!" Mike commanded.

"Now, Mr. Fink" (she always called him "Mr." when he was angry), "what have I done? I don't know, I'm sure—"

"Shut up!" roared Mike. "You...get in there and lay down, or I'll shoot you." Mike swore a great oath, and drew his rifle to his shoulder. Peg climbed into the leafy pile, and Mike heaped crisp leaves over her. Then he hurled a flour barrel crashing to the ground, split a stave into slivers, lit some of them in the fire in the earthbox on the boat, cracking for the evening meal, growling threats that if Peg moved he would shoot her. Now, with the blazing splinters in his hands, he walked around the pile, stooping four times to light the leaves. The wind fanned the flames, and Peg moved uncomfortably.

"Lay still!" thundered Mike.

Peg remained as long as she could, then, screaming, her clothing and her hair blazing, she ran to the shore, leaped into the river. Bedraggled, pathetic, she stood up, water streaming from her. Mike shifted his tobacco, sauntered to the shore.

"There," said Mike, "that'll larn you to be winkin' at them fellers on the other boat."

DAVID CROCKETT.

Bad Scared on the River

The river is an ornery and cantankerous beast of burden, as dangerous as she is useful. Woodsman Davy Crockett once forsook the wilderness trails to try a run down the Obion and Mississippi rivers. He barely escaped with his life!

Some time in the night I was down in the cabin of one of the boats, sitting by the fire, thinking on what a hobble we had got into; and how much better bear-hunting was on hard land, than floating along on the water, when a fellow had to go ahead whether he was exactly willing or not.

The hatchway into the cabin came slap down, right through the top of the boat; and it was the only way out except a small hole in the side, which we had used for putting our arms through to dip up water before we lashed the boats together.

We were now floating sideways, and the boat I was in was the hindmost as we went. All at once I heard the hands begin to run over the top of the boat in great confusion, and pull with all their might; and the first thing I know'd after this we went broadside full tilt against the head of an island, where a large raft of drift timber had lodged. The nature of such a place would be, as everybody knows, to suck the boats down, and turn them right under this raft; and the uppermost boat would, of course, be suck'd down and go under first. As soon as we struck, I bulged for my hatchway, as the boat was turning under sure enough. But when I got to it, the water was pouring through in a current as large as the hole would let it, and as strong as the weight of the river would force it. I found I couldn't get out here, for the boat was now turned down in such a way that it was steeper than a house-top. I now thought of the hole in the side, and made my way in a hurry for that. With difficulty I got to it, and when I got there, I found it was too small for me to get out by my own power, and I began to think that I was in a worse box than ever. But I put my arms through and hollered as loud as I could roar, as the boat I was in hadn't yet quite filled with water up to my head, and the hands who were next to the raft, seeing my arms out, and hearing me holler, seized them, and began to pull. I told them I was sinking, and to pull my arms off, or force me through, for now I know'd well enough it was neck or nothing, come out or sink.

By a violent effort they jerked me through; but I was in a pretty pickle when I got through. I had been sitting without any clothing over my shirt; this was torn off, and I was literally skin'd like a rabbit. I was, however, well pleased to get out in any way, even without shirt or hide; as before I could straighten myself on the boat next to the raft, the one they pull'd me out of went entirely under, and I have never seen it any more to this day.

WILLIAM CARY: *Smoke Boat*, Thomas Gilcrease Institute, Tulsa, Oklahoma

Pirates, Indians and Alligators

In 1832, Washington Irving returned to the United States after seventeen years abroad. He was eager to see the expanding frontier of his native land. He quickly embarked upon an expedition into Indian country west of Arkansas, keeping journals of what he saw and heard. The following is from entries of November 17th.

Saturday Nov 17. Last night ran repeatedly ag[ain]st driftwood — this morng 8 oclock passed thro Stack Island — reach a beautiful broad & long reach of the river.

Here about 20 years since was a formidable gang of river pirates 30 or 40 in number. Kept on an island under the eastern shore called Stack Island & sometimes Robbers' Harbour — ring leader named Mason. The band consisted of outcast Kentuckians, Spaniards, French & c. & c. & c. — well armed — resolute — had boats on the river — horses on the mainland — boarded arks & defenceless boats — noted the cargo — took what they wanted — no resisting them. Some of the keel boats & barges had crews of 40 men well armed — these the robbers dared not attack. The robbers have often been seen by these barges lurking about this island. They could descry boats at a great distance both up & down the river — they had spies in New Orleans. The boatmen & traders had to return by land, by an Indian trail thro the country of the Choctaw natives — several hundred miles — had to cash their merchandise & carry the money

on pack horses. The robbers had trails leading to the great Indian trail. They would way lay the traders & rob them. Seldom killed them unless they fought in defence of their goods. Sometimes when they surprised poor travellers thro mistake they would give them money.

The terror of these robbers spread far & wide. In those days people looked upon an expedition down the Mississippi & Ohio as a fearful undertaking — country wild & unsettled — little known — Indians — river pirates — alligators & c & c & c Long voyage — required hardy and enterprising men — & then the long journey back thro savage tribes & robber hordes —

At length the authorities offered a large reward for Mason's head. He wished to divide his spoil — he had a rival ringleader — they quarrelled about division of spoil. The rival killed him — carried his head to Natchez & claimed reward — a man present who had been robbed on the Indian trail recognized his buttons on the coat of the robber & recognized the latter for one of those who had robbed him. The robber was seized, tried, & hung, and the band was broken up —

The very island has since been washed away by the floods of the river & no trace of the robbers remains, but the pilot who told me this story said he had no doubt that thousands of dollars of the robbers money lay buried about the shore and on the old Indian trail and could be digged up as the country became settled & cultivated.

River Birds

Famed naturalist John James Audubon brought an artist's sensitivity to his description of American rivers. Here is an excerpt from the journals of his exploration of Florida's St. John's River.

The depth of the channel was barely sufficient. My eyes, however, were not directed towards the waters, but on high, where flew some thousands of snowy Pelicans, which had fled affrighted from their resting grounds. How beautifully they performed their broad gyrations, and how matchless, after a while, was the marshalling of their files, as they flew past us!

On the tide we proceeded apace. Myriads of Cormorants covered the face of the waters, and over it Fish-Crows innumerable were already arriving from their distant roosts. We landed at one place to search for the birds whose charming melodies had engaged our attention, and here and there some young Eagles we shot, to add to our store of fresh provisions! The river did not seem to me equal in beauty to the fair Ohio; the shores were in many places low and swampy, to the great delight of the numberless Herons that moved along in gracefulness, and the grim alligators that swam in sluggish sullenness.

JAMES J. AUDUBON: *Snowy Egret,*
National Audubon Society

34

WILLIAM CARY: *Return of the Survey Party,*
Thomas Gilcrease Institute, Tulsa, Oklahoma

River Bile

The river men of the last century exhibited a verve and enthusiasm for expletives that is not to be believed. Truly, in the matter of profanity they waxed sublime. Here, Huck Finn witnesses a virtuoso performance of invective.

There was thirteen men there—they was the watch on deck of course. And a mighty rough-looking lot, too. They had a jug, and tin cups, and they kept the jug moving. One man was singing—roaring, you may say; and it wasn't a nice song—for a parlor, anyway. He roared through his nose, and strung out the last word of every line very long. When he was done they all fetched a kind of Injun war-whoop, and then another was sung. It begun:

> "There was a woman in our towdn,
>   In our towdn did dwed'l [dwell],
> She loved her husband dear-i-lee,
>   But another man twyste as wed'l.
> Singing too, riloo, riloo, riloo,
>   Ri-too, riloo, rilay—e,
> She loved her husband dear-i-lee,
>   But another man twyste as wed'l."

And so on—fourteen verses. It was kind of poor, and when he was going to start on the next verse one of them said it was the tune the old cow died on; and another one said: "Oh, give us a rest!" And another one told him to take a walk. They made fun of him till he got mad and jumped up and begun to cuss the crowd, and said he could lam any thief in the lot.

They was all about to make a break for him, but the biggest man there jumped up and says:

"Set whar you are, gentlemen. Leave him to me; he's my meat."

Then he jumped up in the air three times, and cracked his heels together every time. He flung off a buckskin coat that was all hung with fringes, and says, "You lay thar tell the chawin-up's done"; and flung his hat down, which was all over ribbons, and says, "You lay thar tell his sufferin's is over."

Then he jumped up in the air and cracked his heels together again, and shouted out:

"Whoo-oop! I'm the old original iron-jawed, brass-mounted, copper-bellied corpse-maker from the wilds of Arkansaw! Look at me! I'm the man they call Sudden Death and General Desolation! Sired by a hurricane, dam'd by an earthquake, half-brother to the cholera, nearly related to the smallpox on the mother's side! Look at me! I take nineteen alligators and a bar'l of whiskey for breakfast when I'm in robust health, and a bushel of rattlesnakes and a dead body when I'm ailing. I split the everlasting rocks with my glance, and I squench the thunder when I speak! Whoo-oop! Stand back and give me room according to my strength! Blood's my natural drink, and the wails of the dying is music to my ear. Cast your eye on me, gentlemen! and lay low and hold your breath, for I'm 'bout to turn myself loose!"

All the time he was getting this off, he was shaking his head and looking fierce, and kind of swelling around in a little circle, tucking up his wristbands, and now and then straightening up and beating his breast with his fist, saying, "Look at me, gentlemen!" When he got through, he jumped up and cracked his heels together three times, and let off a roaring "Whoo-oop! I'm the bloodiest son of a wildcat that lives!"

Then the man that had started the row tilted his old slouch hat down over his right eye; then he bent stooping forward, with his back sagged and his south end sticking out far, and his fists a-shoving out and drawing in in front of him, and so went around in a little circle about three times, swelling himself up and breathing hard. Then he straightened, and jumped up and cracked his heels together three times before he lit again (that made them cheer), and he began to shout like this:

"Whoo-oop! bow your neck and spread, for the kingdom of sorrow's a-coming! Hold me down to the earth, for I feel my powers a-working! whoo-oop! I'm a child of sin, *don't* let me get a start! Smoked glass, here, for all! Don't attempt to look at me with the naked eye, gentlemen! When I'm playful I use the meridians of longitude and parallels of latitude for a seine, and drag the Atlantic Ocean for whales! I scratch my head with the lightning and purr myself to sleep with the thunder! When I'm cold, I bile the Gulf of Mexico and bathe in it; when I'm hot I fan myself with an equinoctial storm; when I'm thirsty I reach up and suck a cloud dry like a sponge; when I range the earth hungry, famine follows in my tracks! Whoo-oop! Bow your neck and spread! I put my hand on the sun's face and make it night in the earth; I bite a piece out of the moon and hurry the seasons; I shake myself and crumble the mountains! Contemplate me through leather — *don't* use the naked eye! I'm the man with a petrified heart and biler-iron bowels! The massacre of isolated communities is the pastime of my idle moments, the destruction of nationalities the serious business of my life! The boundless vastness of the great American desert is my inclosed property, and I bury my dead on my own premises!" He jumped up and cracked his heels together three times before he hit (they cheered him again), and as he come down he shouted out: "Whoo-oop! bow your neck and spread, for the Pet Child of Calamity's a-coming!"

Then the other one went to swelling around and blowing again — the first one — the one they called Bob; next, the Child of Calamity chipped in again, bigger than ever....

Both of them was edging away in different directions, growling and shaking their heads and going on about what they was going to do; but a little black-whiskered chap skipped up and says:

"Come back here, you couple of chicken-livered cowards, and I'll thrash the two of ye!"

And he done it, too.

36

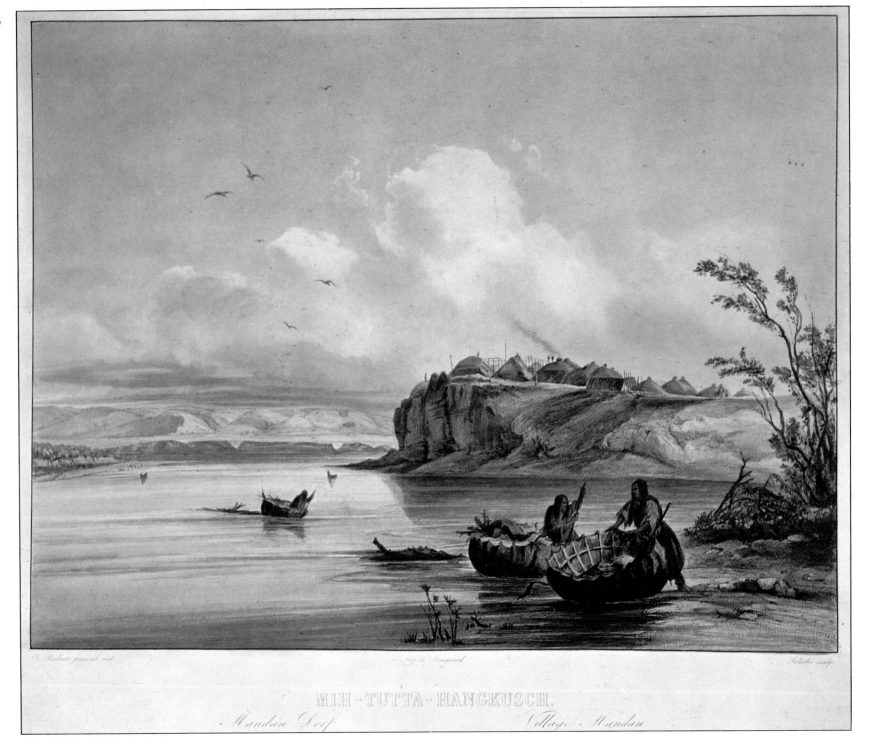

MIH-TUTTA-HANGKUSCH.

Mandan Dorf   Village Mandan.

CARL BODMER: *Bull Boats,*
Thomas Gilcrease Institute, Tulsa, Oklahoma

Mermaids

Long before cities grew up by the rivers, Indian communities fished and played on their banks. George Catlin visited the Minnetarees of the Knife River known as the "People of the Willows." There he was feasted and entertained by "Black Moccasin," chief sachem of the tribe. When Catlin decided that he and his companions should visit other villages, the old chief insisted that one of the young women of his household take them across the river in a bullboat. It proved to be an interesting experience.

When we were in and seated flat on its bottom, with scarce room to adjust our legs or feet, she waded out, pulling it along towards the deeper water, carefully with the other hand attending to her dress, which seemed to be but a light slip and floating upon the surface until the water was about her waist, when it was cast off over her head and thrown ashore, and she plunged forward, swimming and drawing the boat with one hand, which she did with apparent ease. In this manner we were conveyed to the middle of the stream, where we were soon surrounded by a dozen or more beautiful girls, from twelve to eighteen years of age, who had been bathing on the opposite shore. They all swam in a bold and graceful manner, as confidently as so many otters or beavers; and with their long black hair floating on the water, whilst their faces were glowing with jokes and fun, which they were cracking about us and which we could not understand. In the midst of this delightful aquatic group we three sat in our little skin-bound tub (like the "three wise men of Gotham, who went to sea in a bowl," etc.), floating along on the current…amusing ourselves with the playfulness of these creatures floating about under the clear blue water, catching their hands on the side of our boat, occasionally raising half of their bodies out of the water, and sinking again, like so many mermaids.

In the midst of this tantalizing entertainment, in which Ba'tiste and Bogard, as well as myself, were all taking infinite pleasure… we found ourselves in the delightful dilemma of being turned round and round for the expressive amusement of the villagers, who were laughing at us from shore…The group of playful girl swimmers had peremptorily discharged from her occupation our fair conductress who had undertaken to ferry us safely across the river, and they had also ingeniously laid their plans…to exhort from us some little evidence of our liberality, which it was impossible to refuse them after so liberal and bewitching an exhibition…I had some awls in my pockets, which I presented to them, and also a few strings of beautiful beads, which I placed over their delicate necks as they raised them out of the water by the side of our boat; after which they all joined in conducting our craft to the shore…until the water became so shallow that they waded along with great coyness, as long as their bodies could be half concealed under the water, when they gave our boat a last push to the shore, and raising a loud and exultant laugh, plunged back into the river.

Dragon Boat

Not everyone approached the Indians with as much tact as George Catlin. The Western Engineer *was built by the government to explore far up the Missouri and draped with a huge serpent to frighten Indians along the way. Surely it was one of the strangest boats of all time, as described in this contemporary letter.*

The bow of this vessel exhibits the form of a huge serpent, black and scaly, rising out of the water from under the boat, his head as high as the deck, darted forward, his mouth open, vomiting smoke, and apparently carrying the boat on his back. From under the boat at its stern issues a stream of foaming water, dashing violently along. All the machinery is hid. Three small brass field pieces mounted on wheel carriages stand on the deck. The boat is ascending the rapid stream at the rate of three miles an hour. Neither wind nor human hands are seen to help her, and, to the eye of ignorance, the illusion is complete, that a monster of the deep carries her on his back, smoking with fatigue, and lashing the waves with violent exertion. Her equipments are at once calculated to attract and to awe the savages. Objects pleasing and terrifying are at once placed before him — artillery, the flag of the Republic, portraits of the white man and the Indian shaking hands, the calumet of peace, a sword, then the apparent monster with a painted vessel on his back, the sides gaping with portholes and bristling with guns. Taken altogether, and without intelligence of her composition and design, it would require a daring savage to approach and accost her with Hamlet's speech: "Be thou a spirit of health or goblin damned?"

HENRY FARNEY: *Fording the Stream,* Thomas Gilcrease Institute, Tulsa, Oklahoma

Steamboat Round the Bend

Fulton's Folly

On August 17, 1807, Robert Fulton took his steamboat (eventually called the Clermont) *up the Hudson River. Fulton did not invent the steamboat, nor was he the first to demonstrate one successfully — John Fitch launched a steam-powered paddle boat on the Delaware River in 1786. But Fulton did carry the idea further than anyone else had, and he proved the practicality of such craft, showing the way for riverboats that opened up commerce across the United States in the mid-nineteenth century. The following is from a letter Fulton wrote about the* Clermont's *maiden voyage.*

The moment arrived in which the word was to be given for the boat to move. My friends were in groups on the deck. There was anxiety mixed with fear among them. They were silent, sad and weary. I read in their looks nothing but disaster, and almost repented of my efforts. The signal was given and the boat moved on a short distance and then stopped and became immovable. To the silence of the preceding moment, now succeeded murmurs of discontent, and agitations, and whispers and shrugs. I could hear distinctly repeated — "I told you it was so; it is a foolish scheme; I wish we were well out of it."

I elevated myself upon a platform and addressed the assembly. I stated that I knew not what was the matter, but if they would be quiet and indulge me for half an hour, I would either go on or abandon the voyage for that time. This short respite was conceded without objection. I went below and examined the machinery, and discovered that the cause was a slight maladjustment of some of the work. In a short time it was obviated. The boat was again put in motion. She continued to move on. All were still incredulous. None seemed willing to trust the evidence of their own senses. We left the fair city of New York; we passed through the romantic and ever-varying scenery of the Highlands; we descried the clustering houses of Albany; we reached its shores, — and then, even then, when all seemed achieved, I was the victim of disappointment. Imagination superseded the influence of fact. It was then doubted if it could be done again, or if done, it was doubted if it could be made of any great value.

ENTERED ACCORDING TO ACT OF CONGRESS IN THE YEAR 1870 BY CURRIER & IVES IN THE OFFICE OF THE LIBRARIAN OF CONGRESS AT WASHINGTON.

152 NASSAU ST. NEW YORK.

THE GREAT MISSISSIPPI STEAMBOAT RACE

FROM NEW ORLEANS TO ST. LOUIS, JULY 1870.

Between the R.E. Lee, Capt. John W. Cannon and Natchez Capt. Leathers,

Won by the R.E. Lee arriving at St. Louis July 4th at 11:20. A.M.

TIME: 3·DAYS 18 HOURS AND 14 MINUTES.

The Great Boat Race

No single event captures the gaudy excitement that surrounded the river barons and their floating palaces quite like the Great Steamboat Race of 1870. Both the Natchez and the Robert E. Lee were fast boats fired on fat pine and tallow. Their captains were river men of the old school, longtime friends and rivals. And when they raced, the world took notice. Odds were posted in New York, London, Paris, and Berlin. Whole communities turned out for a "plenteous discharge of fire rockets and Roman candles." As the Liberty Tribune reports, the riverfront fairly hummed with excitement.

During the fore part of this week the people of the Mississippi Valley were considerably excited over a race between the steamers R.E. Lee and Natchez, from New Orleans to St. Louis. The levees all along the river swarmed with people from far and near to witness this historical race. The excitement in St. Louis in regard to the great event culminated on the 4th, by the arrival of the R.E. Lee at 11:25 a.m., making the run through, according to the boat's log, in three days, eighteen hours and fourteen minutes. The crowd on the levee was immense, and the river banks was lined with spectators from the bridge piers to Carondelet, six miles, all eager to see the contestants under way, when the Lee hove in sight round the bend.

Below Chouteau Avenue a salute was fired, and as she passed by her landing under full head of steam, forty thousand throats opened and such cheering has been seldom heard. After running up to the bridge to show the spectators her speed, she dropped down to the foot of Walnut Street, and in two minutes was perfectly overrun with thousands of wildly excited people. — The Lee's run beats the late fast trip of the Natchez, three hours and forty-four minutes, and is the fastest on record, not only to St. Louis, but between any two points on the route. The Natchez arrived at 6 p.m., having been caught in a dense fog at Devil's Island, and thereby detained six hours. She also broke a pump on the trip, by which she lost thirty-six minutes, and had considerable trouble with shoal water. It is claimed that the actual running time of the Natchez is eight minutes faster than the Lee's. It is also claimed that all bets on the Lee, after she received wood from the steamer Frank Pargoad, below Helena, are off, as the Pargoad being very fast, applied her power to the Lee for a number of miles, and the race ceased to be a test between the Lee and Natchez, but became one between the Lee and Pargoad. It is said the point is well taken, and the money will not be given up. The precise time of the Natchez has not yet been made up.

River Dandies

*Life on the floating palaces was gay, grand, and devil-may-care.
And why not? As Edna Ferber puts it in the following passage from*
Show Boat, *it was a "last feeble flicker of the picturesque."*

This was the latter '70s, and gambling was as much a part of riverboat life as eating and drinking. Professional gamblers often in-
fested the boats. It was no uncommon sight to see a poker game
that had started in the saloon in the early evening still in progress
when sunrise reddened the river. It was the day of the flowing
moustache, the broad-brimmed hat, the open-faced collar, and the
diamond stud. It constituted masculine America's last feeble flicker
of the picturesque before he sank for ever into the drab ashes of uni-
formity. A Southern gentleman, particularly, clad thus, took on a
dashing and dangerous aspect. The rakish angle of the hat with its
curling brim, the flowing ends of the string tie, the movement of the
slender virile fingers as they stroked the moustache, all were things
to thrill the feminine beholder....

...The Southern men, especially, gave an actual effect of plumes
on their wide-brimmed soft hats as they bowed....

"Well, ma'am, and how are you enjoying your trip on your good
husband's magnificent boat?" It sounded much richer and more
flattering as they actually said it. "...Yo' trip on yo' good husband's
ma-a-a-yg-nif'cent..." They gave one the feeling that they were
really garbed in satin, sword, red heels, lace ruffles.

The Old Lady's Lard

Riverboat racing was no exclusively male pastime. As this nine-teenth-century account by Albert Richardson proves, there were some ladies with as much pride and fire as any man!

Gone forever the era of universal racing, with all its attendant ex-citements — its pet steamers, high wagers, and fierce rivalry!

A good share of American human nature was exhibited by the old lady who took passage, for the first time, on a steamboat, with sev-eral barrels of lard from her Kentucky plantation for the New Or-leans market. Familiar with horrible legends of explosion, collision,

midnight conflagration, she was tremblingly alive to the dangers of her position. She had extorted a solemn promise from the captain that there should be no racing, which relieved her pressing anxiety. But on the second day, a rival boat came in sight, and kept gaining upon them. Their speed was increased, but still, nearer and nearer came the rival until side by side the noble steamers wrestled for victory. Quivering in every tense nerve and strong muscle with the life and will and power that man had given them, they shot madly down the stream.

The passengers crowded the deck. Every pound of steam was put on. The old lady's nerves began to thrill with the general excitement. Life was sweet and lard precious, but what was death to being beaten?

"Captain," she implored, "*can't* we go faster?"

"Not by burning wood," was the reply; "we might with oil."

At that moment the prow of the other steamer darted a few feet ahead. This was too much.

"Captain," she shrieked, "if you let that boat pass us, I'll never travel with you again. Knock open my lard barrels and fire up with *them*!"

The Heyday of the Thimble-Riggers, Dice-Coggers, Strop-Players and Card-Sharpers

Gambling is, was, and probably always will be the chief amusement on the river. Gambling, unfortunately, invites cheating. In this nefarious art the river people proved endlessly inventive. So says John O'Connor, veteran of the golden age of draw poker.

It is said that bottom-dealing was first brought to perfection by a man named Wilson. This desirable consummation was reached in 1834, and about this time first made its appearance on the western rivers, where it was rendered, in the course of a few years, entirely useless, through the blunders of bungling operators, and the verdant learned to protect themselves against the fraud.

The popular game of draw poker, which has entirely superseded straight poker and brag, was the invention of river sharpers, and was first put into practice on the Mississippi steamboats. This game offers to the manipulator a hundred-fold better facilities for fleecing the unwary than either of the old games. The skilful operator can give his victim, with perfect ease, as many big hands as he chooses, and at the same time arm himself or his partner with better ones to beat them. But a shrewd swindler seldom gives a sucker more than an ace-full. He first tempts his appetite two large pairs; then threes of various kinds; after these are expended, he hoists him up a flush or a full hand of a small denomination, and gradually increases them in size till he beats an ace-full for him; beyond this he is not likely to go. Whenever they find customers who will not stand running-up hands, false shuffling and cutting, double discarding is practised upon them; an advantage peculiar to draw poker, and not applicable to any other game. Scores of those who have grown gray in the service of the fickle goddess, and who were the most wary among her votaries, have come to grief through the following artful piece of chicanery:

The partners being seated next to each other, one attends to the betting department, while the latter manipulates the cards. He goes out with three aces, we will say for example, which he conceals in the joint of his knee until it comes his turn to deal. The cards having been dealt, he is ready to help the discarded hands, and he now conveys from their hiding place the stolen cards, in the palm of his hand, and places them upon the top of the pack while in the act of lifting it from the table. These cards are now drawn by his partner, who is informed by a secret "item" of their denomination, and discards his hand accordingly for their reception. As he has the first "say" or "age," and the other players may perhaps not chip in for the pool, it is not necessary to bring out the hidden cards; that is, if any of the players chip in, then he tries, by making a large brag, to run them out; but should any of them prove obstinate and stand the raise, then the three aces are brought into action. The persons who can perform this trick well are by no means numerous.

A Gambler's Punishment

A seasoned cardsharp of the last century christened his biography with the spellbinding title Life and Adventures of Henry Edward Hugunin, or Thirty Years a Gambler: Incidents, Places Visited, Persons Met, With Some Account of Different Games, the Evils of Gambling, and How Never to Lose, Written by Himself. *As one of the evils of gambling, Hugunin recalls that "the way of transgressors is hard," and that on the river "the punishment fit the crime."*

On one trip [on the Mississippi River], on board the *Eclipse* (which was afterwards torn to pieces by a tornado at New Orleans), a man by the name of Smith Mace won $1,000 of a young man, at three-card monte. This being a "sure thing game," and contrary to all the traditions of the sporting fraternity, the winner was looked upon as a thief, and so an indignation meeting was improvised, a committee appointed to institute proceedings, a jury was impaneled, the culprit duly and formally tried, found guilty of violation of all the rules, customs, and proprieties of sporting, and was sentenced either to refund the money at once or to be tied for an hour to the horizontal piston rod, where there would be just room for him to walk back and forth with each movement of the rod. Mace refused to give up the money, and a rope was fastened to the piston rod and tied around his neck in such a manner as to allow him to turn, and he commenced his walk of almost ten feet and back. He only made one remark during the whole hour. After he had walked a while, one of the committee asked him if he would give up the money. He answered, "Go away, I have no time to talk," and he did not have much. It was absolutely necessary for him to keep his eye on the rod and turn exactly with its backward movement or it would have torn his head from his shoulder. He walked his hour, was released, and sent to Coventry for the rest of the trip.

A Real Kentucky Love Letter

Many a lover pined away in the service of the steamboat trade. Gone for months at a time on a river road that stretched a thousand miles, it was not unusual for a man to grow "mighty wrothy" thinking about his girl back home. The following is taken from the New Orleans Picayune.

On board the Steam Boat R.N.O.
March 21st, 1838

Dear Ann,

We are about to shove out, and I have only time to say good-bye. I want you to whip Liza for me before I come back; give her gos. If nothing breaks, in about three weeks, I shall be down again. It makes me mighty wrothy to think I have to go without seeing you. I'd clear my way through the biggest kind of a cane brake to see you any time.

Give my respects to all the family and the gals in particular. The "Wild Bill" has got his steam up, and is fast letting go his cable. So good-bye — off we go. Dont forget your promise, for Gods sake.

Yours until death,
S____ß

Greaser on board St Bt R._____

Buffalo Gals

From the swampy backwater and bayous comes this early American river tune, rendered best by a dozen happy voices and the bright plink of a banjo.

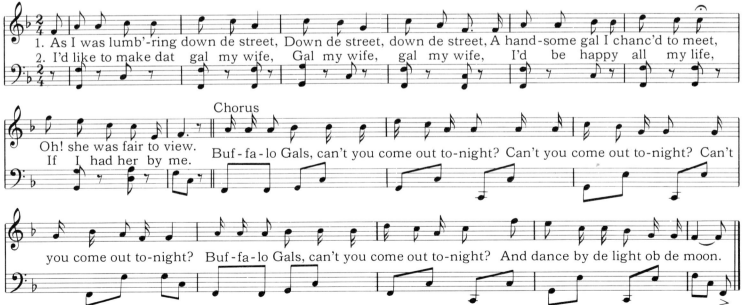

1. As I was lumb'-ring down de street, Down de street, down de street, A hand-some gal I chanc'd to meet,
2. I'd like to make dat gal my wife, Gal my wife, gal my wife, I'd be happy all my life,

Oh! she was fair to view.
If I had her by me.

Chorus

Buf-fa-lo Gals, can't you come out to-night? Can't you come out to-night? Can't you come out to-night? Buf-fa-lo Gals, can't you come out to-night? And dance by de light ob de moon.

Love Boats

It has been called "the oldest profession," but on the river it assumed a new dimension. Here Clark B. Firestone examines those vessels whose principal cargo was lust and liquor.

Over some of the sloughs and the backwaters and swamps that lead off from them there hangs a fading memory and perhaps the ghost of an odor compounded of raw whisky and cheap perfume. In their time the sloughs were part of one of the nation's frontiers. Lawless men have always flocked to the edge of things; but in a mining camp, sooner or later, there was law, even if only lynch law. It was different in the dubious backwaters of the river, for the Mississippi was itself a boundary line between states, and men — and women — whom the law would lay its hand upon needed only to cross from one bank to the other in order to escape jurisdiction.

So there came into being the floating dance hall which was also a saloon and a brothel. It might be just a pair of flatboats joined together and covered with one-story buildings, such as Charles Edward Russell saw as a boy at Davenport and which, as he recites, had "a generic name not to be repeated in print." Thieves, female harpies, and men who would do murder for a meed were aboard these floating dives. Their chosen victims were the rude raftsmen and lumbermen who at winter's end had come out of the valleys of the six great timber rivers in response to the primal urges of lust and liquor. Among the victims was an occasional town inhabitant of better social rank, of the sort that Proverbs characterizes as "a youth devoid of understanding." About the only thing to be said for the predaceous hosts and hostesses is that they used to sing "Buffalo Gals," which is a good song.

With thicker settlement, the floating resorts, also called "love boats," disappeared. They never quite came back, but there was something rather like them during prohibition, and still moonshine is made in sloughs and swampy woods behind some of the islands. Somehow stagnant water and righteous living never got along well together.

Louis Armstrong on the "Dixie Belle"

The showboats, the big proud stern-wheelers churning up the river, gaudy with gilt and gingerbread, alive with the rhythms of river music...it all seems so long ago. But was it? Jazz-master Louis Armstrong recalls his own life on the river and the end of an era.

My river life on [the *Dixie Belle*] (it lasted for two years) is one of my happiest memories and was very valuable to me. It all grew out of a funny accident — another of the breaks I said I have had. Kid Ory's Band had been engaged one evening to play on a truck that was to drive through the streets advertising some big dance. They were always advertising like that with trucks and bands in New Orleans. Well, we were playing a red-hot tune when another truck came along the street with another hot band. We came together at the same corner of Rampart and Perdido Streets where I had been ar-

rested five years before and sent to the Waif's Home. Of course that meant war between the two bands and we went to it, playing our strongest. I remember I almost blew my brains through my trumpet.

A man was standing on the corner listening to the "fight." When we had finally outplayed the other band, this man walked over and said he wanted to speak with me. It was "Fate" Marable, a noted hot pianist and leader of the big band on the excursion steamer *Dixie Belle*. He said he had heard me blow and wanted me for his band. It was in November of 1919. I had been with Kid Ory at the Peter Lalas Cabaret at Iberville and Maris Streets for sixteen months. I had learned a lot from Ory and had begun to get a little reputation, in a small sort of way, as a hot trumpeter. But while I could play music, like most of the others I couldn't read it much yet — just a little. I had made my mind up I wanted to learn.

It may sound funny that I was so quick to leave Kid Ory and sign up for the boat with "Fate" Marable, as though I were just running out on Ory after the big chance he had put my way and all he had done for me. The excursion boats had a big name in those days. They played the Mississippi ports away up to St. Paul and beyond. When they went North on these trips they always had white orchestras, but for the first time it was planned that year to take a colored orchestra along on the *Dixie Belle* when she shoved off in the spring on her trip North. I guess that was because the colored orchestras that had been coming up strong in New Orleans in the last few years, like Kid Ory's, were so hot and good that they were getting a real reputation. The chance to be with that first colored jazz band to go North on the river might have turned any kid's head at nineteen. But even that wouldn't have been enough to make me leave Ory. I wanted to get away from New Orleans for another reason and that was because I was not happy there just then.

Ten months before, when I was eighteen, I got married. I had married a handsome brown-skinned girl from Algiers, Louisiana, named Daisy Parker. We two kids should never have been married. We were too young to understand what it meant. I had to be up most of the night every night, playing in the orchestra, and in that way I neglected her, but I was so crazy about music that I couldn't think about much else. I see now it must have gone hard with a young and pretty girl up from a small town. And was she pretty! She naturally wanted to come ahead of everything else and she had a very high temper, partly, I guess, because she was so young and inexperienced. And in that same way I was quick to resent her remarks, so, as I say, we were not happy — in fact, we were very unhappy, both of us....

Ory knew all about our troubles. He had done his best to help smooth us out, but maybe nobody could have. So when he found I had the chance to go with that fine band on the river for a while, he understood it would be a good thing.

New Orleans, of course, was the hottest and gayest city on the Mississippi then, even including St. Louis, so all through the winter months, from November until April, when the weather is not so hot and New Orleans is at its highest, the excursion boats would stay right there, running dance excursions up and down the river every night and tying up in the daytime.

The steamer *Dixie Belle* was one of the biggest and best of them. She had her berth at the foot of Canal Street. The orchestra would start playing at eight o'clock while she was at the wharf, to attract people, and then she would shove out into the river at eight-thirty every night with a big crowd on board and cruise slowly around until about eleven o'clock when she would come back in. The *Dixie Belle* was fixed up inside something like a dance hall. She was a paddle wheeler, with great paddle wheels on each side, near the middle, and she had big open decks and could hold a lot of people.

So all that winter, which was the winter of 1919 and 1920, we cruised there around New Orleans and every night when we pulled in, of course I would go home to Daisy. Sometimes we were very happy, and I would hate to think of April coming, when I was to go north on the boat.

The orchestra on the *Dixie Belle* was...a twelve-piece orchestra and every man was a crackshot musician. "Fate" Marable had recruited them from the best bands in town, taking this man here and that one there and each one because he was a "hot" player on his own particular instrument. "Fate" was a fine swing pianist himself, and he knew that in time they would learn to play together. Now the most famous jazz orchestras of that day, as you will remember, had had no more than six or seven pieces (though some of the pure brass bands, the marching bands, had more). The old "Dixieland" had only five pieces, and so had Freddy Keppard's "Creole Band." "King" Oliver's famous "Magnolia" and Kid Ory's band had seven pieces each. So, you see, twelve pieces *was* big.

Winter passed and finally April came. The *Dixie Belle* was all cleaned out and fixed up with new paint and polish and finally the day came for us to start up the river. My mother and "Mamma Lucy" came down to see us off, but Daisy wasn't there. We had had another quarrel.

As we pulled out into the river and turned north, I began to feel funny, wishing one minute they'd left me on the wharf and feeling keen the next moment that I was going. The sweeping of the paddle wheels got louder and louder as we got going. It seemed they had never made so much noise before — they were carrying me away from New Orleans for the first time.

In the seven months to come I was to follow the Mississippi for nearly two thousand miles, and visit many places. It was a handful of traveling, believe me, for a kid who'd always been afraid to leave home before.

We shoved away early in the morning so we could make Baton Rouge, our first stop, by night-down. It was a run of about eighty miles, upstream. A few passengers were on board, as it was to be a day trip, although the *Dixie Belle* was not meant to be a boat for regular passenger travel, but only for big excursion parties, so she was not fitted out with many staterooms.

It was a warm spring day and the river was high with water, but not flooding. The musicians did not have much to do except laze around on the decks and watch the shores, or now and then throw a little dice or something. After a while, when we had had our last look at New Orleans, I found myself a nice corner up on the top deck right under the pilot house and settled down with my trumpet and a polishing rag. I had bought myself a fine new instrument just before starting out, but even that wasn't shiny enough for *this* trip. No, suh! So I took the rag and shined her a little and then I put her to my mouth and tried out a few blasts. She sounded strong and sweet, with a good pure tone. I swung a little tune and saw we were going to get along fine together. So then I rubbed her up some more, taking my time, until I was satisfied. Over on the left shore a great cypress swamp was passing slowly by — there must have been hundreds of miles of it, stretching away off to the west — dark and hung all over with Spanish moss. I felt very happy where I was. The sun was just warm enough, the chunking of the paddle wheels was now pleasant to hear and everything was peaceful. Pretty soon I spread the rag on the deck beside me and lay my new trumpet on it and began to think of how lucky I really was. There I was, only nineteen years old, a member of a fine band, and starting out on my first big adventure. And I had my new trumpet to take with me. I reached over and let my hand lay on it, and felt very comfortable....

"Carry On, Old Man River"

Some years ago an elderly retired steamboat captain, Louis Rosché, stood on the banks of the Mississippi at St. Louis, and his thoughts echo the sad joy of all who have shared America's river heritage.

The levee even now was a doomed district, a ghost city which had outlived its day and was existing on borrowed time.

I, too, I reflected, had outlived my time.

But there was always the river! Old as time itself, yet ever young, the great brown surging stream of the Mississippi had been there before there was a city; it would be there after the city was gone. Here was a fitting monument to the glorious old days of steamboating, a mighty monument made of water, yet more enduring than granite.

"Carry on, carry on, Old Man River," I whispered.

I started up the hill toward the city but had to rest every few steps. It seemed as though the hill had grown steeper.

Ol' Man River

Perhaps there are no words that say as much about the deep feeling inspired by the river as those in this Jerome Kern classic.

Lento

Dere's an ol' man called de Mis-sis-sip-pi, Dat's de ol' man dat I'd like to be; What does he care if

Con sentimento

de world's got trou-bles? What does he care if de land ain't free? Ol' man Ri-ver, dat ol' man Ri-ver,

He mus' know sump-in', But don't say noth-in', He just keeps rol-lin', He keeps on rol-lin' a-lon'.

The Twentieth-Century River:
Our American Heritage

"Rivers Are Your Friends"

While still a young man, the author-adventurer Lewis R. Freeman met a character named Swiftwater Bill, with whom he rode a boat full of liquor down the White Horse Rapids in Western Canada. Today it is well to remember Swiftwater Bill's advice.

Good luck, kid. And remember that rivers are always your friends. They take you where you want to go. Don't ever be 'fraid to put your trust in water that's yearning to get home to its resting place in the sea. Remember lil' old Swiftwater Bill told you that, and you'll always be glad for connecting up with him to ride through White Horse on his summer's likker supply.

The Covered Bridge

More than the span of a river, the covered bridge is a distinctly American art form spanning time as well as distance. As Charles Whitney says here, we should cherish those remaining.

The covered bridge rendered great service to the young and growing country. The art of building bridges of stone had already been perfected in Europe but the cost of stone bridges in America was prohibitive. Timber bridges filled the gaps in the transportation system until sufficient capital was accumulated to make possible the construction of permanent bridges.

   The majority of the covered bridges, with their hand hewn timbers stamped with the personality of the pioneers, have gone. Some have burned or rotted, many have been destroyed to make way for modern traffic which they did not contemplate, and others, principally on byways, are still serving the descendants of their builders. It is natural that we should cherish those remaining, not so much for their beauty as for their picturesqueness and human interest. They are distinctly early American, symbolic of the hardiness of our forefathers who built them by hand, and of the greatness of our country which has so outgrown them in a few generations.

Bridge Beyond Belief

I cross this awesome span
The millionth time, and ask myself
What mighty purpose man
Must have in back
Of conscious need, to build
So grand an intertrack?
Could it be because
We ache to humble rivers
In our mortal pride?
Or do we seek some great adventure
On the other side?
Perhaps we merely feel
An urge to render epic poems
Out of steel.
But,
For the millionth time, I answer—
Hang the use!
Mammoth bridges, like mammoth rivers
Are their own excuse.

Edward Cunningham

"You Meet All Kinds on the River"

Richard Bissell, author of Pajama Game *and other Broadway hits, grew up with river water in his veins. He has spent much of his life upon rivers and has written about their every aspect. The following is from* The Monongahela.

You meet all kinds out on the river. On the Monongahela you meet Italians and Poles, and Hungarians and Germans and I don't know what all. Up the Illinois you work with boys from the slums of Chicago and farm boys off the Illinois black dirt country. Up on the Mississippi you meet great-grandsons of the Iowa pioneers, and Swedes and Norwegians from the big northwest country. Down on the Lower Mississippi you're working alongside of Cajuns, who talk a funny lingo, and rough boys from Memphis or New Orleans, who speak with slow and quiet voices. And all this mighty crew of rivermen gang together, they are a breed, like railroaders. Oh, they're not all bold and reckless adventurers — a heap of them are as dumb and drab and spiritless as can be, but in the main they want to go places and do big things out under the sky.

And when the steamboat whistles blow, they put down the beer glass, grab their gauntlet gloves and caps, and go down the bank again and climb onto some old river boat.

And when the whistle blows and they have to get out and make a lock they cuss and moan and claim they're gonna quit. But mostly they stay. That's the way it always was on the river, and the way it always will be, until the Monongahela and the Youghiogheny and the Tygart and the West Branch run dry, and the last steamboat whistle has echoed back off the hills, filling the valleys with that mournful music that haunts you wherever you go.

Angler

The river is the companion of our leisure hours...magic hours as described by A.J. McClane.

Who but an angler knows that magic hour when the red lamp of summer drops behind blackening hemlocks and the mayflies emerge from the dull folds of their nymphal robes to dance in ritual as old as the river itself? Trout appear one by one and the angler begins his game in movements as stylized as Japanese poetry. Perhaps he will hook that wonder-spotted rogue, or maybe he will remain in silent pantomime long into the night with no visible reward.

70

Rogue River Folk

The Rogue River in Oregon is one of eight rivers in the country designated as "wild" by The Wild River Act passed by Congress in 1968. These rivers, or large parts of them, are inaccessible except by boat or foot trail. Charles Hillinger writes of some of the people; the friends of the Rogue River.

The Rogue River sheriff [Allen H. Boice] makes a run up the river from time to time to rescue stranded hikers.

Scores of drift boats, kayaks and rubber rafts are carried on 110-mile runs downstream from Grants Pass to the Pacific Ocean each week this time of year. The river is full of rapids and riffles. Boats overturn. There have been several drownings.

Boice often turns out to help boaters in trouble.

During winter floods, he has rescued residents of remote ranches and isolated river settlements.

Now and then a stray cow gets stuck on a ledge or bar. The Rogue River sheriff rescues the beast.

Roy "Outer Mongolia" Gervais and other riverbank residents radio the sheriff's headquarters in Gold Beach if any problems occur.

"Like people shooting wild game, or hikers or boaters polluting the Rogue or emergencies," explained Boice.

Gervais, 56, comes by his nickname because he's so far up the river, so far away from his nearest neighbors. He lives year around at primitive Paradise Bar Lodge, 7 miles down the river from Marial, as caretaker. Hikers and boaters often spend the night there.

A sign over the Paradise Bar Lodge desk proclaims:

"The world is coming to an end. Please pay now
so I don't have to look all over hell for you."

Near Illahe Riffles, another 12 miles or so downstream, rancher Bill Fitzstephens was moving 100 head of Herefords across the Rogue, one animal at a time, in a cage suspended from a 200-foot cable.

"If Bill drops one in the drink, you know who will be fishin' the cow out of the riffles," said the Rogue River sheriff.

Then he recalled how it was in this area of the river that Hugo the Hermit used to cross the Rogue by jumping along a cable on a makeshift pogo stick.

"Hugo's pogo stick was a forked tree branch," said the sheriff. "The river's 150 feet wide where he crossed back and forth for years, 30 feet above water.

"One day, Hugo and Rogue River rancher Bob Fantz had an argument over a pig. The hermit shot and killed the rancher."

The hermit was found guilty of the shooting and died a few years later in prison.

Larry Lucas, 73, who collects hornets as a hobby, serves family-style lunches out of his turn-of-the-century 10-room house to mail boat passengers and others.

A lifelong resident of the tiny river settlement, Lucas attended Agness School when he was a boy.

"People were more prolific in the old days," said Lucas. "There were 20 kids in school when I was there.

"Now there's only 10. Same school."

Agness hasn't changed much over the years. Neither have any of the other places along the Rogue.

That's why it's a wild river.

"And that's the way we aim to keep her," said Boice.

Tubin' on the Apple River

Charles Kuralt, roving correspondent for CBS News, has traveled all over the country examining delightful bits of Americana. On July 3, 1972, he encountered the Apple River. The following is excerpted from his evening broadcast.

KURALT: This may not look like much to you, but to people around here it looks like money in the bank. This is the biggest industry of Somerset, Wisconsin. What is? This is. Tubin' on the Apple River.

People have gone inner tubing on the Apple for more than 50 years, or as long as there have been inner tubes. But in the last ten years, like everything else in America, tubing has gone big time, and now, Somerset, which has only 729 people, has 15,000 inner tubes, and some summer weekends they're all rented out.

What you do is you go out to a place called River's Edge, four miles up the Apple, get yourself a tube, and head for town. You head for town by sitting down, and letting the Apple River do the rest.

Youths may cavort along the way. Aging correspondents mostly cool it, enjoying the cow and corn country scenery, and the company of veteran tuber Bob Raleigh.

Hey, I think I hear white water behind us. Is this dangerous anywhere along the line?

BOB RALEIGH: Well, it can be if you have a-an extraordinarily large bottom.

KURALT: Then you're going to have trouble.

RALEIGH: Or you don't have a big enough inner tube. From the starting point, oh, for a half a mile or so, it's relatively fast. Once you get down a little ways, the river slows down an awful lot, widens out, becomes very tranquil, peaceful. One could almost fall asleep on the tube. You wouldn't be bothered by anyone, and you'd eventually end up down in Somerset, and somebody'd wake him up. Someone didn't wake him up, the rapids would.

KURALT: Tubing in Somerset, which started in the '20s as a diversion, has become in the '70s an institution, fabled in story and song....Floating down this river it's possible to feel sorry for presidents and kings, who've always had to content themselves with yachting on the Potomac, or punting on the Thames, poor fellows, they never had a chance to go tubin' on the Apple.

White Water

A longtime friend of the river, author James Dickey writes of the joys of running rapids in the backwoods of Georgia.

I concentrated, and the sound of water both deepened and went up a tone. There was another bend ahead, and the river seemed to strain to get there, and we with it.

Around the turn it came into view, and broadened in white. Everywhere we were going was filled with spring-bubblings, with lively rufflings, not dangerous-looking but sprightly and vivid. There was not the sensation of the water's raging, but rather that of its alertness and resourcefulness as it split apart at rocks, frothed lightly, corkscrewed, fluted, fell, recovered, jostled into helmet-shapes over smoothed stones, and then ran out of sight down long garden-staircase steps and around another turn.

I looked for a way through. Drew pointed straight ahead, and it was better done that way than saying it. I sank the paddle into the river. The main current V'd ahead of us, and looked to be straight, as far as I could tell, though the V that indicated the fastest water disappeared about halfway along down the rapids.

"Call the rocks," I hollered. "We want to go straight down the middle."

"Ay, ay," Drew said. "Let's go there."

We headed into the waist of the V. The canoe shifted gears underneath, and the water began to throw us. We rode into the funnel-neck and were sucked into the main rapids so suddenly that it felt as though the ordinary river had been snatched from under us like a rug, and we were tossing and buckling and banging on stones, trying to hold the head of the canoe downriver any way we could. Drew bobbed in front of me, leaping toward a place that could be reached in no other way. He was incompetent but cool; no panic came back from him. Every time he changed sides with his paddle,

I changed to the opposite side. Once we began to go cater-cornered; the water began to swing us broadside like mania, and I felt control sliding away, off somewhere in the bank-bushes looking at us, but Drew made half the right move and I made the other half, and we righted. The hull scraped and banged over rocks, but we hung straight in the current, trembling with force and luck, past the deadly, vibrant rocks we overflowed.

I yelled to Drew to keep his paddle on one side or the other. He chose the right — the biggest rocks seemed to be there; they kept looming up, through the water and just under it — while I alternated between sweeping us forward, adding to our speed wherever I could, and pulling backward on the river whenever we got too close to the rocks on the right. Already it was beginning to be like work I knew, and I felt safer because of that.

Now I could look on past Drew and see the white water lapse and riffle out into green and dark. There was a short flourish of nervous rippling that took us between two black boulders, and we were through....

I was awfully tired, though not sore. As the sun lost energy, so did I, and the edge of night-cold clinched it. I wanted to let go of the river.

We drifted slowly. The current entered my muscles and body as though I were carrying it; it came up through the paddle. I fished up a couple of beers from our pack and opened them and passed one to Drew. He twisted back and took it, one lens of his glasses dark with the sunset.

"It's a hard life with us pioneers," he said, and whistled a line from "In My Birch-Bark Canoe."

I lifted my beer and drank, keeping the beer coming in as fast as I could get it down. The nylon of my legs was drying out and clinging to my calves and shins. I pulled the cloth legs loose from me and took up the paddle again. I felt marvelous.

What Has This Economy Wrought?

Some balance must be struck between the poison and the promise of a technological age. Consumer advocate Ralph Nader urges all friends of the river to seek the answer, lest we bankrupt the heritage of our American waterways.

From the once idyllic rivers of Maine to the Hudson and Delaware Rivers, to the Chesapeake and the Potomac, to the Savannah and the Gulf of Mexico and the Mississippi and Great Lakes, to the Columbia and other waterways of the Pacific Northwest, the tearing down of America into a water wasteland hurtles on.

Water is the most precious, limited natural resource we have in this country. The technology that ruins this water can also save it. But because water belongs to no one — except the people — special interests, including government polluters, use it as their private sewers.

There are many people in this country — old enough to remember when water was a many-splendored thing or young enough to want to have such memories — who want answers.

Kennebec: River Dying

Ecological protest is not so recent as it may seem. The following, by Robert P. Tristram Coffin, first appeared in 1937.

Greed has fouled the Kennebec. The business that does not last, that produces the cheap things which crumble away in the using, has poisoned the great river that sweeps from Moosehead to the sea. Shortsighted men have stripped the finest plumes of the ancient pines from the hills. The beaver and the sturgeon have joined the red men. The tides of silver which used to sweep in with the spring — the shad and herring — are gone for the time. The trout have retreated to the cleaner, smaller streams. The ships and steamboats that once carried life out and over the oldest highway of man are gone. A whole day may go past, and no living human sign pass Fort Popham. The lighthouses turn their anxious eyes around and around and waste their wakefulness on an empty river and ocean.

But the promise of life is still there. The cleanness of snows and rains and vast crystals of lakes are still in the hills ready to restore the river. The shad swim still, all the way up from Florida, eager to enter the Kennebec whenever men say the word. The old nets that hang in the open-chambers may someday be mended and spread out among the June daisies with flakes of silver fish scales starring them. The herring turn their sharp noses each year toward Kennebec's mouth. They would be glad to fill Merrymeeting Bay with treasure once more.

The River Everlasting

Finally what may or may not be the truth, but at least must be the hope of future generations, is eloquently expressed by writer Ward Dorrance.

This was the most heartening of my discoveries: that mill towns fester in one spot while the earth is green around them. The prairies will not be tamed. The hills will not be blasted quite away. The rivers will remain as the first men knew them — the long-browed men whose pipes and spears are locked in caves behind stalagmites. They will reflect our stars. They will mirror our bridges. They will be swift until the last ice.